PAPERMAKING

Susie O'Reilly

With photographs by Zul Mukhida

Thomson Learning
New York

Titles in this series

BATIK AND TIE-DYE
BLOCK PRINTING
MODELING
PAPERMAKING
STENCILS AND SCREENS
WEAVING

Frontispiece *The Japanese use
paper to make all kinds of objects.
Paper fans are popular.*

First published in the
United States in 1993 by
Thomson Learning
115 Fifth Avenue
New York, NY 10003

First published in 1993 by
Wayland (Publishers) Ltd.

Library of Congress Cataloging-in-Publication Data
O'Reilly, Susie.
  Papermaking / Susie O'Reilly ; with photographs by
Zul Mukhida.
      p.   cm. – (Arts & crafts)
  Includes bibliographical references and index.
  Summary: Surveys the history and uses of paper and describes
how to make paper pulp, color paper, and make art with paper.
  ISBN 1-56847-069-X : $14.95
  1. Papermaking –Juvenile literature. 2. Paper, Handmade –
Juvenile literature. [1. Papermaking. 2. Paper. 3. Handicraft.]
I. Mukhida, Zul, ill. II. Title. III. Series.
TS1105.5.074   1993
676 – dc20   93-24397

Printed in Italy.

CONTENTS

Words printed in **bold** appear in the glossary.

GETTING STARTED

We use paper every day, probably without even thinking about it. We write on it, read books made with it, wrap food in it, and recycle it or crumple it up and throw it away. But what is paper?

Paper is made from the long, thin threadlike **fibers** that come from plants and trees. The fibers are beaten to separate them and then mixed with water to form a **pulp**. The pulp is put on a fine-mesh screen called a **mold**, which strains out the water, leaving a sheet of matted fibers on the mesh. Once it is dry this thin layer of fibers is paper.

This basic method is used to make all paper. It is used in industry to make enormous lengths of paper on vast machines. And it is used by individual papermakers producing handmade sheets in small paper mills or artists' studios.

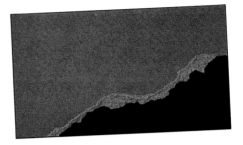

◄ *It is easy to see the fibers in a torn piece of paper.*

The highest-quality paper is made from the long, strong fibers of the inner bark of **hardwood** shrubs (such as mulberry bushes) or from **recycled** cotton and **linen** rags. Since the late nineteenth century, however, most everyday paper has been made from **softwood** trees such as pines and spruces. These trees are grown in forests in such places as Scandinavia, North America, and Indonesia.

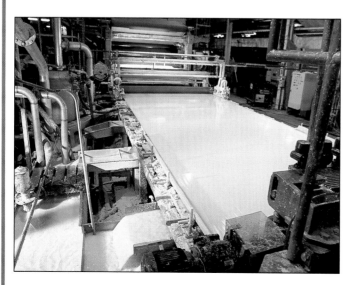

◄ *Most paper is made in paper mills using vast machinery. It is made in rolls, not sheets.*

Making paper by hand using a small mold to form each sheet ►

Paper is more than just a plain, white surface to write on. In recent years many artists have found that, rather than simply painting and printing on paper, they can turn the sheet of paper itself into a work of art. Making paper by hand allows plenty of room to experiment. Paper can be shaped or colored, or have other objects added to it. There are all kinds of interesting possibilities.

The Diver, *by artist David Hockney.* ▶
Hockney worked at a small papermaking studio to produce the sheets for this picture. The design is in the paper itself.

YOU WILL NEED

To make paper pulp
A variety of wastepaper, e.g. computer paper; paper bags; wrapping paper; tissue paper. (Plastic-coated, shiny, or highly illustrated papers are not suitable.)

To make pulp from plants
The leaves and stems of different plants, e.g. rushes; grasses; nettles; the outer leaves of cauliflowers; leaves and stalks of rhubarb; celery stalks; onion peelings; iris leaves.

To make a mold
Nylon mesh (such as curtain netting) with about 100 holes per square inch.

Stainless steel staples and strong stapler
Rustproof nails
A six-foot length of half-inch by half-inch wood
A small saw
A hammer
Waterproof glue

To prepare the pulps
A bucket
A wooden stick
A blender
A plastic washtub
A large saucepan with lid (not aluminum)
An electric or gas burner
Alum (or washing soda)

To make a series of sheets of paper
A shallow rectangular tray
All-purpose kitchen cloths

Two pieces of fiberboard, 10 by 8 inches
Two bricks
A large dropper, such as a turkey baster
A flat-bladed knife
Clean, dry newspaper
An iron
A rolling pin

To color the paper
Tea bags
Instant coffee
Food dyes
Powder paints
Colored paper

General equipment
Apron; rubber gloves; scissors; shears; newspaper for protecting surfaces; thumbtacks; bulletin board.

THE HISTORY OF PAPERMAKING

Around 4,000 years ago, the ancient Egyptians made an early kind of paper using the **papyrus** plant. Parts of the stem of the papyrus were pounded until they were flat, laid out to form a layer, and covered by muddy water from the Nile River. More crisscrossing layers were placed on top. Finally the sheet of papyrus was pressed and left in the sun to dry. The ancient Greeks and Romans also used scrolls made from papyrus. The word "paper" comes from the Greek word *papuros*.

▲ *A piece of papyrus from Egypt, made more than 3,000 years ago. Can you see the crisscross effect made by the strips of papyrus?*

The discovery of a light, flat, smooth surface to write on was enormously important. Despite that, the knowledge of papermaking spread around the world very slowly. This was partly because communication between countries was poor, and also because people who knew the technique kept it a jealously guarded secret.

A picture of early paper-making in China ▼

The Chinese discovered the technique of making paper as we know it today. The accepted date for their invention of paper is A.D. 105. In fact, at around that time many people in China were experimenting to find a better surface on which to write. The Chinese were great **calligraphers**, but found writing on woven cloth or strips of wood and bamboo difficult. Storage was also a problem – bundles of wooden sticks took up a great deal of space.

The Japanese developed the technique of papermaking into a highly skilled craft. Japan is still the country most admired for its hand papermaking. It is mainly a winter activity, carried out by peasant farmers to bring in extra money. Japanese papermakers use a paper mold with a **flexible** bamboo mesh rather than the rigid mesh that is used in other countries. This allows the fibers to crisscross and produces stronger paper.

A Japanese ▶ papermaker using a flexible bamboo mesh

In Europe and North America until the end of the eighteenth century, all paper was made by hand, mainly from rags. Rag-and-bone men used to visit houses with their carts to buy people's cast-off

▼ An early papermaking machine from Europe in the nineteenth century

clothing, which they sold to the paper mills. However, in 1798 the first paper-making machine was invented in France. Machine-made paper was cheap and the demand for it grew. As a result, there were not enough rags to supply the **manufacturers**, who started to search for a new material to turn into paper. The idea of using wood came from the study of wasps. Female wasps chew up old wood to make sawdust. Then they mix it with their **saliva** to make a pulp and form paper nests in which to lay their eggs.

Today ▶ wood from conifer trees is used for paper.

Eventually, it was discovered that fibers from **conifer** trees, such as spruce, pine, and fir, could be used to make paper. This led to an enormous growth in the industry. A much greater range of papers with a wide range of uses could now be produced cheaply.

EXTRAORDINARY USES OF PAPER

Paper can be put to an astonishing number of uses. It was invented because people needed a surface on which to write. Writing on paper is quicker and easier than carving words into stone, clay, or wax **tablets**. However, paper has also been used – and still is used – in many other ways.

The Japanese use paper almost as much as they use fabric. Paper is used to make kites, umbrellas, lanterns, fans, doors, windows, and luggage. The Japanese even make **woven** paper clothing, called *shifu*. A sheet of paper is cut into strips, which are rolled on a stone to make them into threads. These are then woven on a **loom** into cloth. The cloth can be cut and sewn to make **kimonos**, jackets, purses, and other items. Japanese warriors even used paper mixed with other materials to make lightweight armor.

▲ *A paper kimono from Japan*

◄ *In the Far East, paper is used to make umbrellas. This colorful display is in Thailand.*

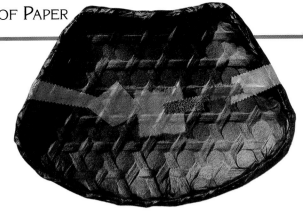

In the nineteenth century, in both Europe and North America, paper was used instead of wood and metal to make many items. People discovered how to make **laminated** panels by gluing sheets of paper together. These panels were waterproof and heat-resistant. They could be sawn into pieces or molded into different shapes. They were used to make coffins, wall panels, cupboards, chairs, and tables, as well as smaller items such as trays and sewing boxes. These objects were painted and then layers of **varnish** were carefully applied to protect the surface and make it smooth.

Today, paper is used to make disposable items. Doctors wear paper gowns and masks when they perform operations. Many babies now wear **disposable** paper diapers. Paper cups, plates, and napkins are used by many take-out restaurants. Most of the things we buy in stores and supermarkets are wrapped in paper.

▲ *Have you used paper plates at a picnic? This beautiful plate is from Japan.*

The world is now using up paper faster than new trees can be grown to produce it. However, the plant fibers used to make paper can be reused. **Environmentalists** have been trying to make people see the need to recycle paper. Recycling is essential, and a certain amount of forest must be left standing. Trees play an important part in putting oxygen back into Earth's **atmosphere** and controlling **climate**. If we continue to cut down trees, the delicate balance of gases that keeps Earth's plants, animals, and humans alive will be destroyed.

◀ *Paper from offices is collected to be treated and recycled (below).*

MAKING A MOLD

A papermaking mold acts like a sieve. It is a frame on which the sheet of paper is formed from the paper pulp. The mold has a fine mesh stretched across it which catches the fibers in the pulp while allowing the water to drain away. A second frame, the same size and shape as the mold but without the mesh, helps to make the edges of the sheets of paper straight. This second frame is called a deckle.

1 Buy a length of wood that is half an inch by half an inch thick. It will have to be cut into four pieces that are 10 inches long and four that are 8 inches long.

3 When the glue is dry, hammer in two nails at each corner to hold the sides in place. **Ask an adult to help you.**

2 Arrange two longer and two shorter pieces of wood to make a rectangular frame. Glue them together with waterproof glue.

4 Find or buy a piece of fine-mesh nylon netting, such as an old net curtain. Cut a piece measuring 10 inches × 12 inches.

5 Wet the netting and staple it to the frame using a large staple gun. Start by stapling the middle of one side, then the middle of the opposite side, pulling as tightly as you can. Then staple the other two sides.

Remember: Always be careful with a staple gun and staples. Ask an adult to help you.

6 Now staple all around the frame, making sure the netting is **taut**. As it dries, it will shrink and become tighter. Cut away any extra netting.

7 Brush around the edges and sides of the frame with a waterproof glue. This will help to hold the netting taut.

8 To make the deckle, repeat steps 2 and 3, using the other four pieces of wood. It must be the same size as the mold.

Note: Papermaking uses a lot of water. It is important to use waterproof glue and nails and staples that will not rust (use ones made of steel, not iron). Rust will mark your paper.

You can also use old picture frames to make the mold and deckle, as long as they are about the same size. The deckle can be a little smaller than the mold, but not larger.

Making Pulp by Recycling Paper

You can recycle almost any kind of paper. Computer printout paper is excellent – it needs to be strong, so it is made from pulp with long fibers. Paper bags and envelopes are also good for recycling.

Avoid any paper with a shiny surface. Shiny papers are coated with clay. This can cause powdery patches on your sheets. It is fine to use paper that has been printed on, including newspaper. However, newspaper does not make very strong paper because it is made of pulp with short fibers. Recycling the paper makes the fibers even shorter.

1 Prepare the paper by removing all traces of glue and taking out any staples.

2 Tear the paper into small squares, about the size of postage stamps.

3 Put the torn paper in a bucket of water and let it soak for at least two hours or, preferably, overnight.

4 Pour off some of the water and use a long, thick piece of wood to beat the paper to a mushy pulp. This can take quite a long time. The pulp needs to be very smooth and creamy.

5 Fill a rectangular plastic tray with water. Pour the pulp into the tray and stir it until it is thoroughly mixed with the water. This is your **vat** of pulp, which is now ready to be made into paper.

6 A quicker method of making pulp is to use a blender. **Ask an adult to help you**. Put a handful of torn paper in the blender and fill it two-thirds full with water.

Replace the lid and hold it down. Blend for 30 seconds. Do this in three bursts of 10 seconds each, resting the machine between bursts. You will need to mix a total of three loads in the blender to make a vat of pulp.

Never pour paper pulp down a sink – it will block the drain. When you have finished using a pulp, drain off the water through fine-mesh netting and then use your hands to squeeze out all the water. Pour the water down the sink and either keep the dry pulp to use later or throw it away in a garbage pail.

MAKING A SHEET OF PAPER

Papermaking uses a lot of water. Be careful not to spill water everywhere.

4 Keeping the mold and deckle level, pull them straight up out of the liquid. Hold them over the vat so that the water can drain back through the mesh.

1 Take a large newspaper and lay it flat on an old table. Now place a small newspaper in the middle. Place a piece of fiberboard on the newspaper. Cover with a damp kitchen cloth.

2 Give your pulp another good stir. Place the mold so that the mesh is face up and put the deckle on top. Grip the two together firmly, holding them by the shorter edges.

3 Slip the mold and deckle at an angle into the pulp mixture. Then straighten them up so that they lie flat beneath the surface of the liquid.

5 Gently shake the mold and deckle backward and forward and from side to side. This will help the fibers to settle. Do not overdo it, or your sheet of paper will be uneven.

6 Take away the deckle and transfer the mold to the prepared newspaper pad, turning it over so that the pulp side faces down on the kitchen cloth.

7 In one gentle movement, press one edge of the sheet of paper onto the kitchen cloth, lift up the opposite edge of the mold, and take it away. The sheet should have transferred to the kitchen cloth. You have made your first piece of paper!

You may need a few tries before you manage to get an even layer of pulp on the mesh and then turn it out as a single sheet. If things go wrong, you can remove the pulp from the cloth by laying the cloth on top of the pulp in the vat.

HELPFUL HINTS

1 Use a large dropper (a turkey baster is excellent), full of pulp mixture, to fill in any areas where the sheet of paper is thin.

2 Straighten the edges of the sheet of paper by gently pushing the edges with the side of a flat-bladed knife.

Turn to pages 12-13 and 18-19 for information on making paper pulp.

COUCHING, SIZING, AND FINISHING

COUCHING

"Couching" is a special word used by papermakers. It describes the process of transferring a sheet of newly made paper onto a drying cloth or board, pressing it, and drying it. This is how you make a series of sheets of paper. Try working in pairs – one of you as vatperson and one as coucher.

1 Place a damp kitchen cloth on top of the first sheet of paper. Smooth out all the wrinkles. Any creases will show up in the sheets of paper you make.

2 Make more sheets of paper and put them on top of one another, placing damp cloths between each. Continue until you have made five sheets.

3 Cover the last sheet with a damp cloth. Take a second piece of fiberboard and place it on top. Place two bricks on the board and leave for fifteen minutes.

4 Put a sheet of plastic over a large, flat surface (a table or an area of floor that people will not walk on). Spread a thick layer of newspaper over the plastic sheet. Remove the top board and carefully peel off each kitchen cloth with its sheet of paper. Do not worry about damaging the sheets – the damp paper is very flexible.

5 Leave the sheets on the newspaper to dry. This will take between 12 and 24 hours. Change the newspapers whenever they become soaked. Drying the sheets in a warm room will speed up the process.

SIZING

"Sizing" does not mean cutting the paper to the correct size! In papermaking, sizing means treating paper to make it strong and **nonabsorbent**, so that ink and paint do not soak into the surface and make a blot.

Here are several ways of sizing. Waxed and oiled papers are not suitable for writing on, but they are strong and have an interesting surface.

1 Mix a tablespoonful of waterproof glue into a jar of water. Stir it thoroughly until all the lumps are gone. Add this to your paper pulp *before* you start making the paper.

2 Paint both sides of a sheet of paper with a thin coat of vegetable oil. This will make it **translucent**.

3 Coat the paper with wax. Put some wax candles in an old tin can and put the can in a saucepan, half full of water. Heat the pan of water on an electric or gas burner until the candles melt. Brush the melted wax over the paper using an old brush.

Ask an adult to help you melt the wax. Do not let the water boil dry.

FINISHING

You can give different **finishes** to your paper. Here are some ideas.

1 If you want your paper to have a rough surface, let the sheets dry out completely before gently peeling them away from the cloths.

2 If you want the paper to have a smooth, even finish, roll each sheet with a rolling pin while it is still slightly damp.

3 Dry your paper under weights to make sure it dries absolutely flat. Two bricks placed on a board make good weights.

MAKING PAPER FROM PLANTS

As well as recycling wastepaper, it is possible to make paper from plants. Plants with long, narrow leaves, such as rushes, reeds, corn plants, and irises, or stringy stalks, such as rhubarb, celery, parsnip, and sunflowers, are particularly suitable.

Try to use plant matter that would otherwise be thrown away. For example, you can use vegetable peelings, such as onion skins and outer cabbage leaves. If you live near a market, you might be able to get some more unusual leaves, such as the tops of pineapples. The plants you use will depend on the time of the year and what is available.

Producing paper from plants is slightly more complicated than recycling old paper because the plant matter must be broken down first to release the fibers.

▲ *Paper made from plants: (clockwise from top left) coriander and daffodil petals; pineapple tops; celery and fennel; iris.*

1 Collect your plant matter. You will need to fill a plastic washtub halfway.

2 Remove any woody stems or really tough stalks. Cut the rest into pieces about 2 inches long.

3 Dissolve an ounce of alum in cold water and pour it into a large, old saucepan. Do not use an aluminum pan. Fill the pan three-quarters full with water.

4 Add your plant matter. Make sure it is completely covered by the water. Put a lid on the pot and place it on a gas or electric burner. Bring the liquid to a boil, turn down the heat, and simmer very slowly. **Ask an adult to help you do this. Watch very carefully to make sure that the pan does not boil dry. Open windows and doors to allow steam to escape.**

5 After three-quarters of an hour, check to see if the plants are ready. Ask an adult to remove a small amount of the plant matter from the pot and squeeze it. If it comes apart or feels very soft it is ready.

Remember that tough plant matter, such as pineapple tops, will take longer to soften than other matter, such as cabbage leaves and rhubarb stalks.

6 Put a piece of netting over a plastic tub in a sink. Pour the liquid and plant matter into the tub. Pick up the edges of the material and let the liquid run through. Gather up the material to make a small bag and hold it under running water. Keep it under the faucet until the liquid running out is clear.

7 Some plant matter turns brown from the alum. If this happens, put some bleach in a bowl, add cold water, stir well, and add the plant matter. The bleach will lighten its color. After an hour, pour the material into a piece of netting and rinse under the faucet. **Be careful not to splash the bleach around or on yourself. Ask an adult to help you.**

8 The plant matter now needs to be beaten to make a smooth pulp – just like pulp made from recycled paper. Turn to pages 12-13 for instructions on how to do this. Many plant papers shrink and buckle as they dry. Dry them under weights to keep them as flat as possible.

Always be careful with stove burners. Ask an adult to help you with them.

MAKING COLORED AND TEXTURED PAPERS

You can add color and **texture** to your paper in many different ways.
Experiment to get the effects you want.

ADDING COLOR

1 Make a cup of tea using a tea bag. Leave the bag in the water for at least a quarter of an hour and squeeze it with a spoon. Add the tea to your pulp. Ordinary tea will produce various shades of brown. A cup of coffee will produce a slightly darker shade of brown. Camomile tea will make a soft yellow, and, surprisingly, fruit teas will make shades of gray.

2 To make bright colors, add some pieces of colored paper when you make your pulp. The **dye** in it will color the pulp. Paper napkins give very good colors. You can mix colors together – for example, yellow and red napkins together produce a shade of orange.

3 To make even brighter colors, mix powdered paints with a little water and stir them into your pulp.

4 Try using natural dyes. For example, onion skins boiled in water give a range of soft orange colors. Add the water to your pulp.

▼ *Papers made using different colorings: (clockwise from top left) curry powder; onion skins; tea leaves; instant coffee; (center) powdered paints.*

ADDING TEXTURE

1 When you have made your pulp, add other objects to it. Try flower petals; leaf skeletons; seeds; tiny pieces of ribbon; threads of silk, cotton, or wool; pieces of metal foil; or scraps of other papers.

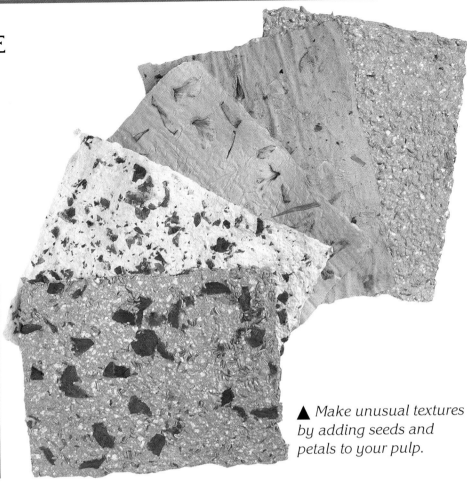

▲ *Make unusual textures by adding seeds and petals to your pulp.*

2 Leave your paper to dry on a textured surface, such as a piece of tweed fabric or a lace mat.

3 Instead of using a piece of plain netting as a mesh on your mold, try a piece of patterned lace.

4 **Stamp** objects into the damp paper to make a raised pattern. This is called **embossing**.

MAKING A WALL HANGING

Papermaking can be an art in itself. Use what you know about making paper to produce a work of art with a special message or meaning. For example, if you make pulp from the needles of your Christmas tree, the paper you make will remind you of Christmas. If you recycle an old address book, the finished sheets will have a special meaning for you. Make sure other people understand the meaning of your work by carefully choosing the color, texture, and edges you create. Give your work a title that hints at its message.

1 Spend time thinking about your picture and how you can get your ideas across through paper.

2 Look at the work of other artists – painters, sculptors, photographers, and craftspeople. See how they use color, texture, and titles to get their ideas and feelings across.

3 Collect paper samples and make sketches of things you see to give you more ideas. Study the textures of different objects.

4 Decide what materials you want to use, collect them together, and make your pulp.

▲ *These hangings are called* Christmas *and* A Summer's Day. *The summer piece is made from garden plants. The Christmas piece is made from wrapping paper and the colored foil from crackers.*

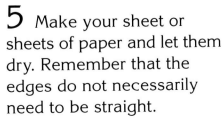

5 Make your sheet or sheets of paper and let them dry. Remember that the edges do not necessarily need to be straight.

6 Now hang your work so that it can be displayed. Hang it on a bulletin board or mount it on a large sheet of stiff paper.

MAKING A PAPER BOWL

Damp sheets of newly made paper are very flexible. If a sheet is pressed over a solid object, it will take on that shape itself when it dries. This method of making **three-dimensional** objects is called "casting."

1 Find a plastic or china bowl the size you would like to make your paper bowl. You can mold the paper either on the inside or the outside of the bowl.

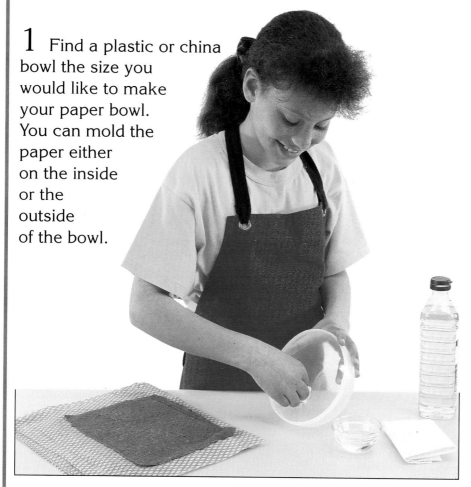

4 Press several layers of damp paper into the bowl. Use a spray bottle to dampen the sheets of paper with water if necessary.

2 Put a few drops of vegetable oil on a paper towel and wipe the surface of the bowl. This will make it easier to remove the paper shape later.

3 Make some sheets of paper. If you want to make a large bowl, you will need to use a large picture frame as your mold when you make the sheets.

5 Fold down the edges of the sheets of paper inside the rim of the bowl or leave them ragged. Let it dry out completely.

6 When the paper is dry, slip the molded paper bowl out of the plastic or china bowl.

FINISHING

There are lots of different ways of finishing the bowl. Here are some ideas.

1 Varnish the paper bowl inside and out and let it dry. Paint on another two or three coats, letting the varnish dry between each coat.

2 Brush several coats of vegetable oil on the inside and outside of the molded bowl.

3 Coat the bowl with wax (see page 17). You can add extra pieces of paper to the surface and rim of the bowl and use the wax to seal them on.

▼ *Make a variety of items using different bowls and plates.*

INVESTIGATING PAPERS

Collect as many different kinds of paper as you can find. You should be able to find examples of **newsprint**, writing paper, airmail paper, white and brown envelopes, greaseproof paper, tracing paper, waxed paper cartons (for soup or milk), cellophane candy wrappers, Christmas wrapping paper, brown wrapping paper, paper handkerchiefs, tissue paper, a disposable diaper, blotting paper, shiny paper, wallpaper, and recycled papers (including some you have made yourself). Try to include some Japanese paper from an art shop and paper with a **watermark**.

1 **Absorbency** Put a little water in a saucer. Place each paper in turn on the water. Do any soak up the water?

Most of the papers listed above have particular uses. They have different qualities that make them suitable for the job they do. For example, disposable diapers and facial tissues need to be soft and absorbent. A milk carton must not leak. Writing paper needs a nonabsorbent surface to hold the ink. Brown wrapping paper needs to be strong.

Now test your paper samples. Try these experiments and carefully note your results on a chart.

2 **Translucency** Hold the papers up to the light. Can you see through them?

3 Watermarks Hold the papers up to the light. Can you see a word or pattern?

4 Coating Try writing on the different papers with an ink pen. If the paper is not coated, the ink will sink into the surface. If the paper has a lot of coating, the ink will sit on the surface and smudge easily.

5 Rattle Well-made paper has what is known as a good "rattle." Hold a piece of paper in one hand and flick it with the fingers of your other hand. Can you hear the different sounds the various papers make?

6 Texture Shut your eyes and run your fingers lightly over the different papers. What do the different surfaces feel like?

7 Strength Try tearing each of the papers. How easy is it? Can you make a straight tear? Most machine-made papers have a **grain**. The machine has rollers that make all the fibers lie the same way. It is easier to tear along the grain than across it, so to do this test properly try tearing the paper in both directions.

	blotting paper	wrapping paper	tracing paper	sketchbook paper	recycled paper
					✓
handmade		✓	✓	✓	
machine-made	✓			✓	✓
absorbent	✓				
translucent			✓		
watermarked			✓	✓	✓
coated		✓	✓	✓	
uncoated	✓				✓
good rattle		✓		✓	
texture				✓	✓
tears across	✓		✓	✓	✓
tears down		✓	✓		✓

THE GALLERY

Handmade paper has special qualities. It may have an interesting surface texture or uneven edges. Other natural and handmade objects have similar qualities. Look around. Notice edges and rims. Look for **weathered** objects. Take photographs and collect pictures to paste in a notebook. Use your collection as a source of ideas for your papermaking.

These pictures will give you some ideas. The ones on this page show interesting textures. The ones on the opposite page will give you ideas for edges.

◀ *Weathered stone*

▲ *The skin of citrus fruit*

▼ *Rusty metal*

▼ *Sea spray*

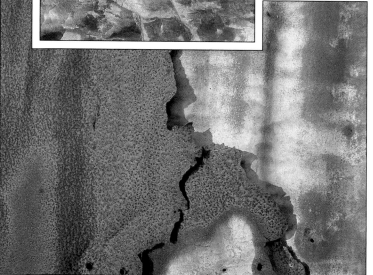

▲ A shoreline

▲ A fluffy cloud

◀ The edge of a leaf

▼ A line of cliffs

GLOSSARY

Atmosphere The air that surrounds the earth. It is made up of different gases.

Calligraphers People who are very good at writing by hand. To calligraphers, beautiful writing is an art.

Climate The type of weather that usually occurs in a particular part of the world.

Conifers Trees, such as pines, that have evergreen leaves and produce cones.

Disposable Intended to be thrown away after use.

Dye A substance, usually a powder or a liquid, that is used to color fabric, paper, or other materials.

Embossing Making a raised pattern on a flat surface, usually by pressing something into it.

Environmentalists People who work to protect the environment. The environment is the natural surroundings – on land, in water, or in the air – in which plants and animals live.

Fibers Tiny, thin threads that make up the stalks, stems, and leaves of plants and the hairs of animals. Plant fibers are used to make paper and other materials.

Finish The surface texture of a material such as cloth or paper.

Flexible Able to bend without breaking.

Grain The general direction of the fibers in a piece of wood or paper.

Hardwood Wood from trees such as oaks and beeches that has a hard, close-grained texture.

Kimonos Traditional Japanese robes.

Laminated Bonded together into sheets.

Linen Woven fabric made from flax plants.

Loom A frame used in weaving.

Manufacturers People or businesses that make goods, usually on a large scale.

Mold In papermaking, the frame on which a sheet of paper is made. It has a fine screen stretched across it which catches the pulp and strains out the water.

Newsprint The special name for the paper that newspapers are printed on.

Nonabsorbent Unable to soak up liquids.

Papyrus A tall, reedlike plant.

Pulp A soft, soggy substance.

Recycled Treated and processed to be used again.

Saliva The liquid in an animal's mouth that makes food easier to swallow.

Softwood Wood from trees such as conifers that has a loose, open-grained texture.

Stamp To press down to make a mark.

Tablets Slabs of stone, clay, or wax used for writing on before paper was invented.

Taut Extremely tight.

Texture The feel of an object's surface.

Three-dimensional Having three dimensions: height, width, and depth.

Translucent Allowing light to show through.

Varnish A clear, sticky liquid that can be painted on an object. When it dries it becomes hard and shiny.

Vat A large container for holding liquids.

Watermark A mark put on paper that can only be seen when it is held up to the light. Watermarks are put on banknotes to make them difficult to forge.

Weathered Worn away by the weather.

Woven Made by weaving – interlacing threads to make a kind of grid.

FURTHER INFORMATION

BOOKS TO READ

Brown, James C. *Papercrafts for All Seasons.* (Carthage, Ill.: Fearon Techer Aids, 1984).

Condon, Judith. *Recycling Paper.* Waste Control. (New York: Franklin Watts, 1991).

Langley, Andrew. *Wood.* Resources. (New York: Thomson Learning, 1993).

Readers Digest Crafts & Hobbies. (Pleasantville, N.Y., 1979).

Wood, Tim. *Making Paper.* (New York: Franklin Watts, 1988).

USEFUL ADDRESSES

American Forest and Paper
  Association
260 Madison Avenue
New York, NY 10016

American Forest Council
1250 Connecticut Ave. NW
Suite 320
Washington, DC 20036

Save America's Forests
4 Library Court SE
Washington, DC 20003

PLACE TO VISIT

The Dard Hunter Museum
  of Paper
Massachusetts Institute of
  Technology
Cambridge, MA

For further information about arts and crafts:

American Crafts Council
72 Spring Street
New York, NY 10012

INDEX

ACKNOWLEDGMENTS

The publishers would like to thank the following for allowing their photographs to be reproduced: Bridgeman Art Library 5 (Bradford City Art Gallery and Museums); Cephas 4 bottom right; Eye Ubiquitous 4 top, 9 top, 28 bottom left; Michael Holford 6 left; Tony Stone Worldwide frontispiece (A. Diesendruck), 8 left (A. Cassidy), 28 top left (L. Valder), 28 top right (R. Weller), 28 bottom right (P. Berger), 29 top (J. Garrett), 29 upper middle (D. Wilson), 29 lower middle (R. Siegal), 29 bottom (O. Benn); Topham 7 top, 8 right, 9 bottom right; Wayland Picture Library 4 left (A. Blackburn), 6 right, 7 left, 9 bottom left (A. Blackburn); Zefa 7 bottom right.

All other photographs, including cover, were supplied by Zul Mukhida. Logo artwork throughout the book was supplied by John Yates.

The Diver (one of two) by David Hockney, on page 5, appears by kind permission of the artist: © David Hockney 1978.

The author would like to thank Jan Peek of Liberty Junior School, Merton, and Jackie Lee and Sarah Mossop of The Crafts Council for their help.